MW01287053

DISCLAIMER: This information entertainment purposes only and is not the place of any medical, legal, financial, traditional psychological, or other professional advice. Kelli McCray/One Mind and Spirit Brand is not responsible for your choices you make using this material. Success depends on the integrity of your workings, the initial conditions of your life and your natural abilities so results will vary.

Thank you to my Beloved Spiritual Guide Wisdom for guidance in my personal life and assisting others for over 30 years. Thank you Wisdom for bringing the children! Even though I was always told I was here to work with children, I never in my wildest dreams knew it would be on a spiritual level and to this magnitude…but the babies have been coming for almost 10 years now, waiting to be heard and healed with their sacred baths. I Am still amazed to this day! I am so honored Wisdom that you chose to work with me, through me and for me. I Am Grateful.

Thank you to Asha Sims, Donna Parker, Barjohn Lee, John Roddy and Queen Azima Lok for your continued love, encouragement, nudges, nags and support. I love you for and through it all. I Am Grateful.

Thank you to the hundreds and hundreds of clients who have participated in this journey with me and with their spiritual baths, who have experienced healings and life transformations during this sacred process. What a blessing! Thank you for saying YES, to yourselves, your healing, and becoming brand new! I AM Grateful.

CONTACT INFORMATION
Kelli McCray

www.onemindandspirit.com

Copyright 2018 Kelli McCray/One Mind and Spirit Brand

All rights reserved.

ISBN:1727184831
ISBN-13:9781727184839

John 5:4 KJV

For an Angel went down at a certain season into the pool and troubled the water. Whosoever the first after the troubling of the water stepped in was made whole of whatever disease he had..

Table of Contents

What is a Natureceutical?

NATURCEUTICALS — A Term Created By Wisdom

NATURE - Products of the Earth; the natural world

CEUTICALS - A product designed to work in or on the body; supports the idea of self-care; maybe manufactured or organic substances although may not be regulated by law.

Introduction

Hello. I invite you to wade in the water! I invite you to bathe in warm water with sustenance from the Earth - Natureceuticals. Here you will journey to the time that shaped your foundation, your early years. A time before becoming the adult who you are today. The adult today who tends to hold on to emotions/thoughts/beliefs like: fear, anger, heartache, rejection, regret, abuse, embarrassment, unworthiness, lies of not being loved, not valued, not deserving of... just to name a few things. These emotions/thoughts/beliefs are usually formed and shaped in the foundational years and reside within as layers, like an onion. This means, we are using the emotions/thoughts/beliefs of our past experiences to move through the activities and events in our present life. We need to be reborn and rebirthed to react a new way, hence, Wisdom's customized spiritual bath journey is used for this process. This spiritual bath can be very healing and will assist in removing layers of the onion. There is not a limit to the number of baths that can be taken, although they should be spaced out at least 2 weeks to allow for the work done with the bath to adjust and acclimate within you. This spiritual bath can cleanse, heal, and release at a cell level. It can even transform the memories in your cells where damaging emotions/thoughts/beliefs have been stored. This is what will provide you the opportunity to look and/or feel differently after you are done with this spiritual bath process.

I invite you to take a journey for yourself, within yourself. Take your Spiritual Support Team (your Angels, Loved Ones and/or Spirit Guides) with you to your childhood safe place. It is the most sacred space of all safe places. Here you can create more love, joy, wholeness, healing and prosperity for yourself. More importantly, you will establish a divine relationship with your spiritual team that assures you that you are never alone. I invite you to anoint, restore and reset your soul. You will be grateful for this journey!

Chapter 1

Who is offering this blessed invitation?

I am Kelli McCray. I am an Intuitive Life Coach, Oracle, Medium, Shaman, Reiki Attuned, Nontraditional Ordained Minister. For 30 plus years, Wisdom (my Spirit Guide) and I have been in an intimate partnership with my intuition and life. We connect with you, the client, and whom chooses to represent you: The Angels, Spirit Guides and/or Loved Ones. In session, they ALL will be present, but they will communicate one at a time. Along with providing clear, concise and accurate information about you, Wisdom will also take me to your child self or younger self. When the child/younger self shows up, they want to heal and be free. They want to reveal the place(s) that have you "stuck" in your life today. These stuck places are the wounds that create the holes in your spirit. These wounds are your emotions/thoughts/beliefs from childhood or the younger self. It's alright that you don't remember this time of your life, that is for your protection, but the effects are still there. The holes in your spirit can create challenges, obstacles, and pain, loss of feelings, confusion etc. These effects of these wounds/holes are still influencing the experiences in your adult life today. There is a simple, safe and wholesome solution. It's a Spiritual Bath or what we call Wading in the Water with Natureceuticals! These recipes are soothing balms to heal the holes within your spirit. The bath water, anointed with Natureceuticals is an elixir for creating a new life and a new beginning. Healing and releasing these wounds or holes of your past is a powerful transformation for wholeness and your spirit on all levels.

During an intuitive consultative session, Wisdom channels customized bath prescriptions. These Natureceuticals integrate with your life experience, your spirit and offer healing during the spiritual bath process. The water, herbs, spices and/or fruit are synonymous with the experiences that need healing. It is a recipe that penetrates the soul, bringing forth peace, wholeness and well-being. The recipes have been used by hundreds, upon hundreds of clients.

Chapter 2

What is A Spiritual Bath?

Our lives begin in the water, our mother's womb. Sometimes our soul will still cry to return to this place of safety, warmth, comfort and love especially when life becomes dark or burdened. When our spirits are worn, a Spiritual Tune-up is necessary. A great tool for this a Spiritual Bath.

There is nothing like a good bath! Spiritual Baths will reset our total being mentally, physically and spiritually. These sacred baths are set with an intentional purpose usually with prayer and/or affirmation, even though the spoken word alone will suffice. The spiritual baths prescribed by Wisdom are set with intentions for healing, protection, love, restoring, cleaning, releasing and/or rejuvenation of the spirit. For Wisdom's spiritual baths *NO MUSIC* OR SOAP IS ALLOWED. (see later chapter) The recipes for a spiritual bath prescribed by Wisdom are intended to take you on a journey of SELF, that offer healing. With an open heart, relax in the tub and journey with your spirit to help usher in your better and greater self.

If you don't have a tub or you are not able to get into a bathtub, a foot bath for a minimum of 30 minutes with the Naturceuticals added in the water will offer the same beneficial treatment. Please remember to wrap a blanket or wrap around you if using the foot bath

Chapter 3

Things Not To Do In Wisdom's Spiritual Baths

We all love a good song to stir our emotions and our souls! As beautiful as music is, it can be a hindrance to Wisdom's spiritual bath. Since this type of Spiritual Bath is for healing and an inward journey, a certain song may often trigger memories of a very difficult time in life. Some experiences may not be remembered until a certain song is heard! This may create an extremely painful turbulence for your bath. These turbulent and triggered emotions may hinder you from going within and/or working closely with your spiritual support team. Therefore, music can influence how deep you go on your journey with yourself, inhibit going deeper within yourself, create fear and feeling unsafe to meet/spend time with your younger self, interfere with working with your spiritual team, create unnecessary discomfort, and even block receiving any messages that may be given to you from your spiritual support team. It is ok to sing a song, especially if it is a song that you remember to be comforting. If that is the case, you are probably being urged to sing by your spiritual support team like a parent or grandparent. Singing is also another form of releasing using the Throat and Heart Chakras.

Please do not use soap for this or *any* spiritual bath. If you feel you are not clean, you may shower **BEFORE** your bath. Please do not take a shower after your bath. Taking a shower **AFTER** the bath will wash everything that is working on your behalf down the drain. It is best to air dry or lightly pat yourself dry.

Chapter 4

Things You May Feel or Notice During Wisdom's Spiritual Bath

- You may fall asleep. You really won't be asleep, but a form of meditating. You are working on yourself at a deep level.
- Losing track of time, especially feeling as if in the tub a long time
- Anger, sadness or crying, followed by joy and excitement. This happens after what no longer serves you has been released.
- Profuse sweating
- Feeling someone is touching, hugging or with you. Hearing someone speaking to you.
- The water heating up or never gets cold.
- Seeing bubbles or a substance floating in the water other than initial ingredients. It may be black, white, slimy or greasy.

- Being drained or exhausted after you get out of the tub, then rejuvenated after you rest.
- Unexplained happiness/joy/excitement
- Smells from your past - other than the ingredients in the water.
- A strong or great release to have a bowel movement or vomit

Remain open as your experience may bring some new feelings, thoughts and emotions. Each person and each bath, even for yourself is different

Chapter 5

The Basis for ALL of Wisdom's Customized Baths
(can be used alone as a spiritual bath or combined with the other ingredients)

1. *Pink Candle*

2. *Lemons* (cut in half, then cut in half again, giving you eight quarters)

3. *Handfuls of Epsom Salt* (this is more than enough)

Pink Candle:

The pink candle symbolizes self-love and God's (Universal) love for you. They also help with deprogramming old thoughts and feelings that are embedded within our cells. The flame is the transformer. It ignites what is within us. It clears away and purifies negative energy, while activating the new seeds for our life to be born. The flame gives courage and strength. The size of the candle does not matter, nor whether it has fragrance.

Lemons:

Lemons are a catalyst to activate the other herbs. Lemons also symbolize the human heart. The yellow color brings optimism by lifting the vibration of the soul. Lemons help you move through transition as they are Illuminators of Truths. They remove blockages; open spiritual paths and removes negativity; a natural cleanser. Lemons hold qualities of purification, love and healing. In addition, the seeds represent new beginnings. The fragrance is calming and elevates a sense of wellbeing. The number 8 is for Balance.

Epsom Salt:

The body, mind and spirit are united with three handfuls of Epsom Salt. Salt is of the Earth, therefore Epsom Salts allows you to ground and raise your vibrational energy. It cleanses at a cellular and auric level. It holds the weight of the toxic energy being released and carries it down the drain. Detoxification of the body, mind and spirit helps to open space in our being for more of the things we desire. Physically, Epsom Salt relaxes our muscles and calms our nerves.

Chapter 6

Wisdom's Herb/Spice Bath List

Allspice- Uplifts vibrations; Increases energy and determination. Works on higher vibrations; A catalyst in all healing mixtures.

Anise- Good for bringing about changes in attitude; Helps to refocus thoughts; Assists with emotional balance; Encourages the conscious mind to open to the Universe; For love, protection and blessings.

Apple Juice- Apple is associated with the Soul. Aids strength. Provides peace, clarity, hope and happiness; Motivates one to take better care of self; Alleviates worry, doubt and reoccurrences of toxic emotions such as anger, jealousy, fear, feeling vulnerable and feeling morally wrong. *(use One Half Cup)*

Basil- An Angelic Herb; Dispels melancholy, grief, hatred; Provides clarity and understanding; Helps with processing what is fact or fiction; Provides peacemaking with self or others; Clears negative energy and pains of the past; A trust and confidence builder; Uplifts; Provides balance and harmony to allow light to illuminate the soul; Encourages self love and courage.

Black Pepper- For comfort, endurance, flexibility; Provides fearlessness, motivation and/or strength to venture forth; Allows Guardian Angels to bring protective elements into our lives; Helps us to reunite with our spirit after long term neglect; For quickening when mixed with other herbs.

Cherry Juice – Brings honesty; Used when someone needs to snap out of finding fault, being pessimistic, has self-pity, determined to remain upset, negative, or has a heavy spirit. Elevates sadness and unhappiness. *(use One Half Cup)*

Cinnamon- Helps us find inner love; Transforms sadness into happiness; Clears trapped emotions from past trauma; Provides warmth, protection, strength, joy and a sense of comfort; Increases spiritual mood and energy; Brings realization that love is always here for us; Provides assurance that help is at hand when we need it.

Clove- Acts as a catalyst when used with other herbs. Eases fears, dispels negativity; For protection and regeneration; Improves memory/focus; Stirs the spirit into action to help us move forward; Awakens senses to know angels are near; Raises spiritual vibration; For protection and Love.

Coriander- Gently stimulates action for a new life and seek new horizons; Helps us to look deeper at truth; Helps us slow down when making changes; Offers love, protection, healing, enthusiasm, optimism, sincerity, uplifting.

Dill- Can diffuse a situation; brings together all the current aspects of life; Helps us to look at painful situations easier; Brings Compassion for self; Calms; Harmony; Tenderness; Love; Protection. Helps bring in the Angels. (Can use dill pickle juice)

Ginger- For liberation, optimism, healing, love. Provides courage to break out of fear; Encourages being a free spirit in thought or action. Stimulates and protects; Warming; Angelic Herb.

Honey- Honey is Holy, it binds the other ingredients; Brings forth the sweetness in life; Happiness; Soothing; Creates a sweeter attitude; Ushers in love, joy and healing.

Hyssop – An angelic and holy herb; Awakens the heart and brings acceptance; For removal of emotional uncleanliness, guilt and fear; Purifying for those that believe they have actions that need to be forgiven; A cleansing and protection herb.

Lavender - Creates a calm/relaxing atmosphere; Shields negativity; Lifts weight of depression and sadness; Brings emotional balance; Allows us to know we are never alone; Removes indecisiveness and emotional conflict; Happiness, Love, Peace, Comfort and Protection.

Orange Juice - The Joy and Positivity fruit; Brings happiness to the heart and spirit; For enthusiasm, hope and love; For self-pity; Banishes melancholy; Angelic Fragrance. *(use One Half Cup)*

Peppermint - Possesses strong healing vibrations; Stimulates, calms and soothes the spirit; Eases thoughts of hopelessness; Helps connection with inner self; Heals and purifies; Releases negativity; Heightens a clearer perception; Used to generate change and get things moving.

Pineapple Juice – For contentment with Self; Builds confidence; Honesty; Aids shyness; Releases poverty consciousness mindset; Feelings of being judged or comparing self to others; helps to be more outspoken;

Enhances clarity of being on the right path; Helps raise personal power. *(use One Half Cup)*

Rose - Promotes healing, feeling safe and unconditional love for self. An Angelic fragrance; Comfort and peace; Confidence booster; Balance, protection and harmony; Happiness.

Rosemary - an Angelic herb; Helps the person to know they are supported and not alone; Rids negativity; Helps shift to optimistic energy; Awakens the heart; Provides mental clarity and focus; Cleansing, healing and purifying.

Strawberry – Releases feelings of guilt; Aids to leave a dysfunctional childhood in the past; Builds self worth; Very grounding. *(Use Blender to Liquify Frozen or Fresh totaling a One Half Cup – you may add a little water for blending)*

Thyme - An Angelic herb; Energetically allows spiritual support; Aids healing; Helps release emotions and traumas from the past. For grief; Provides strength and courage; Balances mind and spirit; Releases fear and false beliefs; Encourages positive actions; Dispels negativity.

Vanilla - Increases self love; Enhances feelings of inner peace; Calms and soothes; Promotes a happy and healthy environment; Healing and comforting; Lowers defensive guard; Vitalizes energy; Warming; Strengthens the mind.

Vinegar - Clears out negative energies; Improves personal views; Eases inability to connect with others on an intimate level; Helps release long held issues which have an influence on life; Draws energetic debris and toxins out of the body and aura. *(use One Half Cup White or Apple Cider Vinegar)*

Ylang Ylang – Although mostly known for being an aphrodisiac, it is energetically attuned to Love; Dispels fear and apprehension; Helps with releasing guilt and other negative emotions such as jealousy, anger, frustration which prevents someone from moving forward; Assists with increasing self-worth and confidence; Relaxes the body and spirit to release feelings of anxiety.

Kitchen cabinet spices, for example thyme, basil, cinnamon, are perfect to use. Spices like Cloves or Star Anise may be used whole or ground. Follow your inner guidance to know the appropriate amount of herbs/spices to use in your bath unless a definite amount is noted. There is not a right or wrong, but what is comfortable for you and your spirit. You may place the herbs/spices in the tub naturally, or you may use organza bags, stockings or cheesecloth to avoid additional cleanup. Please *DO NOT* use an ingredient if there is a known allergy. Some ingredients may affect a pregnancy – Please Do Not Use if pregnant.

Chapter 7

10 Examples Of Client Baths and Testimonies

(not edited; words in the client's own language)

BATH #1

Basis of a Pink Candle, 2 Lemons and 3 handfuls Epsom Salt

Maraschino Cherry juice (can use regular cherry juice)

Basil

3 Peppermint Teabags

Vanilla

Black Pepper

TESTIMONY OF BATH: I am grateful for my experience with Wisdom...my lesson was about growth and finding my purpose. I have really grown in my journey. I have set goals and I have a plan. I have found my purpose which is encourage, teach, inspire and uplift others. I am now on my path to fulfilling my goal. I am learning more about myself spiritually, and as I learn I am teaching which encourages, uplifts and inspires others I meet on my journey. Because of Wisdom's words to me, I am enrolled at the Charlotte Spirituality Center where classes will begin in January. I've enrolled in a 3 year program, but my focus is one step/day at a time...at graduation, I will be a Spiritual Director...helping others on their journey. My experience has given me a dream, a goal and a plan which I am putting into action...I am GRATEFUL. Much love

Bath #2:

Basis of a Pink Candle, 2 Lemons and 3 handfuls Epsom Salt
Thyme
Cinnamon
Honey (or Brown Sugar) 1/4 to 1/2 a cup (amount specific to this person)

TESTIMONY: Out of all the spiritual things I've done for learning and/or healing, this bath was the most powerful experience I have ever had! I worked with my child self and my spirit guide talking about many things from my past and past hurts that I was holding on to. It was comforting to know I was not alone. I prayed. I cried. I sweated profusely and cried some more. After the bath, the most amazing things happened to me. I felt a great sense of release. **Release** of a belief about myself that had a major impact and holding me back from having the life I wanted. I also felt so refreshed. **Refreshed** because the release had made me feel like a new person and finally I felt **Renewed**. I was filled with a fresh sense of optimism and energy about myself and for my life. I have started many new projects and now paid my worth.

Bath # 3

Basis of a Pink Candle, 2 Lemons and 3 handfuls Epsom salt

3 Peppermint tea bags

1 cup Orange Juice

½ cup Turmeric (for banishing and protection)

½ cup Brown Sugar

3 tsp. Cinnamon

1 tsp. Black Pepper

1 tsp. Rosemary

Instructions: Sit in the bath and meet my inner child in India. She will be leaning against a camel waiting for me.

When I began to gather the ingredients for my bath I immediately felt a surge of energy which made me anxious, it was like my inner child knew I was preparing to meet with her. Once I got into my bath I began to talk to her, I closed my eyes and envisioned that I was with her as she leaned against this camel. I let her talk. I let her say all the things she no longer wanted to carry. I let her cry and I let her lean against me, I stroked her head as she lay in my lap and just cried her little heart out and I even cried with her at moments. Once she calmed down, I began to assure her that we were one, and we were in a good place. I explained to her that she could be all she wanted to be, she could be free, she could be loved and loving, she could rid herself of adult situations, that I had her best interest and she could trust me to handle our life the rest of the way. I explained to her that it wasn't her fault or responsibility and she was allowed to be free. We walked for a long time, then she let me walk her closer to the light. When we got there she was excited to go but afraid to leave me. I assured her again that I love her with every fiber in my being, that I will always be true to her, and that I needed her to release me and myself so we could both be free and live the life we're destined to. She hugged me tightly, kissed me on my cheek and ran off into the light. I stood there for a moment, watching her run into the light. Almost unable to move, I didn't know what to do now that I could feel her gone. I did feel the release. I burned Rosemary to clear my house instead of sage as instructed. I meditated and sat for a good hour as the feeling of peace washed over me. I felt free, I felt clarity, I felt grown, I felt amazing, I felt like someone hit a switch and I could see things from an elevated perspective. Previous harmful habits or thought patterns immediately revealed themselves. It was like I could suddenly make sense of all the nonsense we had created. I still feel I have a lot of work to do but I feel I'm able to do so from a better state of mind and spirit. Thank you for helping me set a part of me free.

Bath #4

*Basis of a Pink Candle, 2 Lemons and 3 handfuls Epsom Salt

Basil

Black pepper

3 Peppermint tea bags

Honey

Cinnamon

1/2 cup Pineapple juice

TESTIMONY: I met my inner child at my safe place, aunt's house. She was waiting with an apron at the kitchen table. I had a conversation with my inner child thanking her for helping me get to this moment in my life. I told her that I appreciate her, she is loved and is loving, beautiful, smart and she makes good decisions. I told her it's okay to speak her truth and she has a lot to say and it is time to be heard. I let her know she is safe and protected and what happened in the past is not and was not her fault. She was not to blame for all the adult situations and irresponsibility that happened around her. I explained everything is ok and she can trust me to take over now. I promised I wouldn't let her down. I will see her dreams through and make sure we become the woman that she has always wanted to be. But she's got to trust me to do that. She smiled at me proudly and agreed.

We walked hand in hand for a little while and then I watched her walk away into the clouds. I felt as light as a feather after I got out of the water. I felt a happiness I couldn't explain. I really released that little girl! I feel centered, calm, and focused. Even when things get tricky, I respond as an experienced woman who knows things are working for my good instead of panicking like a child who is afraid of the unknown. I feel a strength I have never felt. Thank you

Bath # 5

Basis of a Pink Candle, 2 Lemons and 3 handfuls Epsom Salt

2 Oranges (cut in 4 quarters)

Cinnamon

Basil

Vinegar

TESTIMONY: I was going through a transition point in my life, I went to see Kelli to gain clarification on the direction I was planning to take. The experience was very powerful and transforming. The reading gave me conformation on a lot of the feelings and emotions that I had been feeling up to that point. Through the reading with Wisdom, I was instructed to take a spiritual bath with specific ingredients added in order to cleanse myself of a lot of grief, guilt and resistance I had placed in my path. After taking my bath, I felt renewed and whole. I made calls to some loved ones to clear past anger. I applied for jobs I never thought I was capable of getting even though my credentials said I was more than qualified. I actually was hired at my dream job! I walk in peace clarity and joy now. My session with Wisdom was linked toward gaining enlightenment to my existence by convening with my higher self. Thank you, Kelli, Wisdom, and the Most High for sharing your gift.

Bath # 6

Basis of a Pink Candle, 2 Lemons and 3 handfuls Epsom Salt

White Vinegar

Honey

Cinnamon

Releasing the younger self that endured a bad relationship.

TESTIMONY: I stepped in my bath with the intention of releasing anything that was not for my highest good. I relaxed and meditated for a while on the things I needed to let go. I spoke to my younger self, apologizing for not always nurturing her and for even abandoning her at times. I asked for her forgiveness and then released her to the Light with one of my guides. When ended my bath with, "As I step from this bath, I leave behind all energy that does not serve my path and I draw to myself light and love". I experienced a sense of lightness and calm when I stepped out of the water, but I realized much later that the cleansing was not complete; it had only just begun. I noticed within that next hour that my throat was a bit scratchy and I felt slightly sluggish. The following morning those symptoms persisted and I discovered that my temperature was slightly elevated. By evening, I was feeling somewhat congested and my fever had risen to 101 degrees. Over the course of the next few days, although I had no aches or pains, my temperature reached as high as 104 degrees and I was so congested that I went through two full, large boxes of tissues and had to ask someone to bring me two more. I had never blown my nose so much in my life and I couldn't recall ever running a fever that high as an adult. Besides the stuffy nose, I experienced very little discomfort and I simply allowed myself to rest, sleeping more than usual. By the 6th day, my symptoms had resolved and I returned to my usual routine. I am so grateful that the bath allowed me to purge so much so quickly. I was able to release energy that had been blocked for many years. Thanks to Kelli and Wisdom.

* Fever: Anger. Burning up.

*Flu: Responding to mass negativity

* Head Cold – Backed up tears that have not been cried. The tears have backed up into your sinus cavities which holds resentment and grief. The backed up and blocked tears effect the ability to breathe properly.

*Scratchy/Sore Throat – Holding words of Anger

Bath # 7

*Basis of a Pink Candle, 2 Lemons and 3 handfuls Epsom Salt

3 Peppermint tea bags

2-3 spoons of Allspice

Honey

Vanilla

Basil

Black Pepper

1-2 cups of Apple Juice (specific to the client)

TESTIMONY: This was the first spiritual bath I ever took. I was VERY nervous during my inner child reading and in the spiritual bath because I didn't know what to expect. But Kelli's gentle, loving energy put me at ease as the reading went on. The fear was all in my head. Kelli answered all of my questions that I didn't even have to ask, it was like she was reading my mind. I was very shocked that I had an inner child, and that I abandoned her! And I was even more shocked when Kelli said apple juice as one of the ingredients of the bath, that was my favorite childhood drink. After the reading, I felt so much guilt and sadness for leaving my little me behind, and it became obvious that I hadn't healed from my childhood disappointments like I thought.

I doubted I was powerful enough to communicate with my child self and my Spirit Guide. As I slowly relaxed in the water, I saw myself riding my bike in my childhood neighborhood. It was so freeing to coast down the big hill and feel the breeze. As I continued, I realized that I was riding to my house, and this is where we met. When I arrived, I saw my Spirit Guide. I was terrified to meet my child self, so I collapsed on the grass pulling my spirit guide's arms telling her, "no I'm too scared to face her, I don't want to do this." She had me repeat an affirmation that I am safe and I eventually got off the ground and walked to the front steps of my childhood house where my child self was sitting there waiting for me.

Still in the tub, we talked for over an hour. Little Me was so sweet and loving. I told her how grateful I was for her and how she made me into the woman I am today. I told her how smart, pretty, and loved she is, and apologized for leaving her behind. I cried so hard, it was like everything I experienced as a child hit me at once. I felt all of those old emotions release again. My Spirit Guide came back and my little me said she was ready to go now. She left holding my Spirit Guide's hand. I didn't want to let her go, but I had to. I finally was reunited with her, and now she had to leave. After the bath, I felt much lighter, and more connected to my own emotions. Emotions that I denied, I was now feeling, I was going through the dark night of the soul. I was able to channel my spirit guide after the reading, and she helped me through the tough emotions I had after the bath. Instead of falling victim to those emotions like before, I was actually beginning to heal them. They arose not for me to feel, but for me to heal and release them. I'm so thankful to have met Kelli. Her healing sessions gave me new energy and vision to live a more positive, love filled life, free from childhood disappointments I once harbored.

Bath # 8

Basis of a Pink Candle, 2 Lemons and 3 handfuls Epsom Salt

Basil

Rosemary

1 cup of Orange juice

Vanilla

Cinnamon

TESTIMONY: In the tub go back to my grandmothers back yard. This was my safe place as a child, my grandmother's house. I see my child self in the backyard and I have a conversation with her. I told my child self "Thank you... I love you... you are safe, protected, and provided for. It's not your fault and I apologize you had to deal with adult experiences. It's ok to have a voice and to speak up. It's ok to be honest. It's ok to speak your truth. You are safe to speak your truth."

During the bath as I was speaking to myself I felt like burdens were being lifted off me. I felt relaxed, my mind felt at ease, and I felt more secure with myself. Since my spiritual bath, I have noticed that I deal with different types of situations more with ease and I have been able to speak my truth much easier than it was before the bath.

Bath # 9

Basis of a Pink Candle, 2 Lemons and 3 handfuls Epsom Salt

Cinnamon

4 Peppermint Tea bags

Black Pepper

Lavender

TESTIMONY: My first spiritual bath and the experience was incredible! I met with my child self. We had a beautiful conversation. After I sent the pain and the guilt I was carrying for years into the love and light, along with my child self I started sweating profusely from the top of my head. My hair was soak and wet. It was a major release. I feel so much better with feeling free and peace. Thank you.

Bath # 10

Basis of a Pink Candle, 2 Lemons and 3 handfuls Epsom Salt

Rosemary

Thyme

Basil

Lavender essential oil

Bath to Detox Emotionally

I had within me what I call my warrior princess. She was my younger self that rose up to protect and defend me when she thought it was necessary. I also had a lot of pinned up energy that resulted in constant anger and defensiveness. I had also finally left a job I was unhappy working and had experienced constant betrayal and zero support. I, along with my Spirit Guide met with my younger self to communicate. I told her she was safe, protected and didn't have to fight anymore. That she is loved and loving and supported. That the decisions she made were the best that could be at the time with the knowledge and resources she had. She is responsible and smart. That she is not alone. We talked, hugged and cried. This bath along with some other work I had started doing helped me reach another level of peace and joy. I am grateful.

Made in the USA
Columbia, SC
29 April 2021

37058268R00028